NEW HAMPSHIRE

The Granite State

BY
JOHN HAMILTON

Abdo & Daughters
An imprint of Abdo Publishing | abdopublishing.com

abdopublishing.com

Published by ABDO Publishing, a division of ABDO, PO Box 398166, Minneapolis, Minnesota 55439. Copyright © 2017 by Abdo Consulting Group, Inc. International copyrights reserved in all countries. No part of this book may be reproduced in any form without written permission from the publisher. ABDO & Daughters™ is a trademark and logo of ABDO Publishing.

Printed in the United States of America, North Mankato, Minnesota.
042016
092016

Editor: Sue Hamilton   **Contributing Editor:** Bridget O'Brien
Graphic Design: Sue Hamilton
Cover Art Direction: Candice Keimig   **Cover Photo Selection:** Neil Klinepier
Cover Photo: iStock
Interior Images: Alamy, AP, Brian Blackden, Comstock, Dartmouth College, Dreamstime, Getty, Granger Collection, Gunter Kuchler, History in Full Color-Restoration/Colorization, iStock, John Michael Wright, Library of Congress, Manchester Monarchs, Manchester-Boston Regional Airport, Mile High Maps, Minden Pictures, NASA, New Hampshire Fisher Cats, One Mile Up, Rob Gallagher, and Seacoast United Phantoms.

Statistics: *State and City Populations*, U.S. Census Bureau, July 1, 2015/2014 estimates; *Land and Water Area*, U.S. Census Bureau, 2010 Census, MAF/TIGER database; *State Temperature Extremes*, NOAA National Climatic Data Center; *Climatology and Average Annual Precipitation*, NOAA National Climatic Data Center, 1980-2015 statewide averages; *State Highest and Lowest Points*, NOAA National Geodetic Survey.

Websites: To learn more about the United States, visit booklinks.abdopublishing.com. These links are routinely monitored and updated to provide the most current information available.

Cataloging-in-Publication Data

Names: Hamilton, John, 1959- author.
Title: New Hampshire / by John Hamilton.
Description: Minneapolis, MN : Abdo Publishing, [2017] | Series: The United States of America | Includes index.
Identifiers: LCCN 2015957621 | ISBN 9781680783315 (lib. bdg.) | ISBN 9781680774351 (ebook)
Subjects: LCSH: New Hampshire--Juvenile literature.
Classification: DDC 974.2--dc23
LC record available at http://lccn.loc.gov/2015957621

CONTENTS

THE GRANITE STATE

When people first came to New Hampshire, they were attracted to the state's treasure trove of natural resources. Huge white pine trees were prized for making ship masts. There was plenty of farmland, wildlife, and fish. Fast-moving rivers provided power for mills and factories.

Since colonial times, the rugged people who settled New Hampshire have always been independent minded. That attitude continues today. The state's motto is "Live free or die." Citizens are quick to tell you what's on their minds, from maple syrup recipes to politics. Every four years, New Hampshire is the first state to hold presidential primaries to select the nation's Republican and Democratic candidates.

New Hampshire's bedrock is made of granite. The rock is hard and strong, just like the state's people. That is why New Hampshire today is nicknamed "The Granite State."

A New Hampshire resident votes in the state's presidential primary. Every four years, New Hampshire is the first state to hold a presidential primary.

QUICK FACTS

Name: New Hampshire is named for the southern English county of Hampshire.

State Capital: Concord, population 42,444

Date of Statehood: June 21, 1788 (9th state)

Population: 1,330,608 (41st-most populous state)

Area (Total Land and Water): 9,349 square miles (24,214 sq km), 46th-largest state

Largest City: Manchester, population 110,448

Nickname: The Granite State

Motto: Live Free or Die

State Bird: Purple Finch

State Flower: Purple Lilac

State Rock: Granite

State Tree: White Birch

State Song: "Old New Hampshire"

Highest Point: Mount Washington, 6,288 feet (1,917 m)

Lowest Point: Atlantic Ocean, 0 feet (0 m)

Average July High Temperature: 79°F (26°C)

Record High Temperature: 106°F (41°C), in Nashua on July 4, 1911

Average January Low Temperature: 8°F (-13°C)

Record Low Temperature: -50°F (-46°C), on Mount Washington on January 22, 1885

Franklin Pierce

Average Annual Precipitation: 47 inches (119 cm)

Number of U.S. Senators: 2

Number of U.S. Representatives: 2

U.S. Presidents Born in New Hampshire: Franklin Pierce (1804-1869)

U.S. Postal Service Abbreviation: NH

GEOGRAPHY

New Hampshire is part of a six-state region called New England, which is in the northeastern part of the United States. It is a small state, measuring 9,349 square miles (24,214 sq km). It ranks just 46th in size among the states.

New Hampshire is shaped like a long triangle pointed northward. The Connecticut River forms a long border with the state of Vermont to the west. To the south is Massachusetts. To the north is the Canadian province of Quebec. Maine is to the east, plus an 18-mile (29-km) section of Atlantic Ocean coastline. It is the shortest ocean coastline of all the coastal states.

The Connecticut River forms a border between New Hampshire and Vermont.

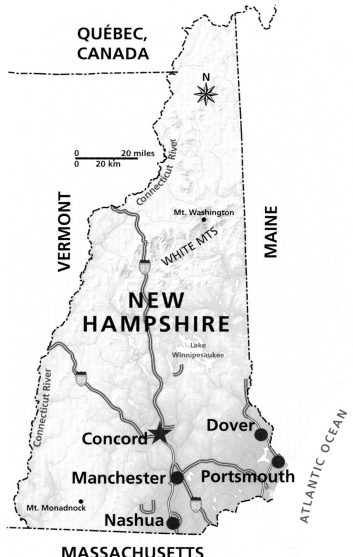

QUÉBEC, CANADA

N

VERMONT

Connecticut River

Mt. Washington

WHITE MTS

MAINE

93

NEW HAMPSHIRE

Lake Winnipesaukee

Connecticut River

89

Concord ★

Dover

Manchester

Portsmouth

ATLANTIC OCEAN

Mt. Monadnock

93

Nashua

MASSACHUSETTS

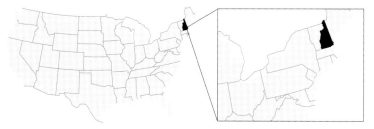

New Hampshire's total land and water area is 9,349 square miles (24,214 sq km). It is the 46th-largest state. The state capital is Concord.

The tallest peaks in New Hampshire's White Mountains are named after presidents.

The rugged White Mountains are part of the Appalachian Mountains. They are in the northern part of the state. They probably got their name because of the exposed white granite of their peaks. The beautiful Presidential Range is part of the White Mountains. Its tallest peaks are named after United States presidents. Mount Washington is the tallest mountain in New Hampshire, and in all of New England. Its summit soars 6,288 feet (1,917 m) high.

South of the White Mountains is a region called the New England Upland. There are low mountain ranges and river valleys that are fertile for farming. Lake Winnipesaukee is in this part of the state. It is the largest lake in New Hampshire. A popular tourist destination, it is 21 miles (34 km) long, covers 69 square miles (179 sq km), and has more than 250 islands.

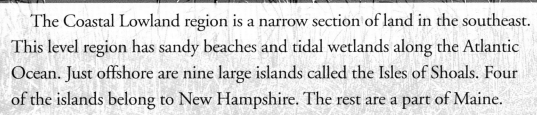

The Coastal Lowland region is a narrow section of land in the southeast. This level region has sandy beaches and tidal wetlands along the Atlantic Ocean. Just offshore are nine large islands called the Isles of Shoals. Four of the islands belong to New Hampshire. The rest are a part of Maine.

There are approximately 1,300 lakes in New Hampshire, and 40,000 miles (64,374 km) of rivers and streams. The state is nicknamed "The Mother of Rivers." The Androscoggin, Cocheco, Connecticut, Merrimack, Saco, Salmon Falls, Pemigewasset, Piscataqua, and Winnipesaukee Rivers all begin in New Hampshire. Three major cities—Manchester, Nashua, and Concord—lie along the Merrimack River. The Connecticut River Valley has rolling hills and plenty of good farmland.

CLIMATE AND
WEATHER

New Hampshire has a humid continental climate. There are four distinct seasons, with big swings in temperature between summer and winter. Summers are mostly warm and humid, while winters are cold and wet. Milder weather occurs near the Atlantic Ocean. The average temperature drops in the higher elevations of the White Mountains.

When large air masses collide over the region, extreme weather can occur. Cold, dry air often sinks down from Canada. Warm, moist air blows from the south. Cool, humid air arrives from the Atlantic Ocean. The weather in New Hampshire is affected by the sea breezes, ocean currents, and tall mountains. Thunderstorms and blizzards can strike. Luckily, tornadoes are rare.

A lightning strike in Hampton, New Hampshire.

A hiker fights against the wind on Mount Washington. A wind gust of 231 miles per hour (372 kph) was recorded on the summit in 1934.

Some of the world's worst weather occurs on Mount Washington. Blinding snow, bitter cold, ice, and fog are common. New Hampshire's record low temperature was recorded on the mountain on January 22, 1885. That day, the thermometer plunged to -50°F (-46°C). In 1934, a weather station on top of the mountain recorded a surface wind gust of 231 miles per hour (372 kph), the strongest ever recorded in the Western Hemisphere. By comparison, a Category 5 hurricane—the strongest—has winds of 157 miles per hour (253 kph) or higher.

CLIMATE AND WEATHER

PLANTS AND
ANIMALS

The Granite State is 84 percent covered by forests, the second-most in the nation (behind Maine). That is about 4.8 million acres (1.9 million ha) of forestland. New Hampshire's forests are prized for logging, recreation, and tourism. They also provide wildlife habitat.

Spruce and fir forests are found in northern New Hampshire. There are also balsam, white cedar, and tamarack trees. The woodlands of central and southern New Hampshire have a great variety of trees, including white pine, maple, beech, ash, aspen, and oak. White birch is the official state tree of New Hampshire. The state is famous for its spectacular fall colors, especially in its deciduous forests in the south. The leaves turn bright red, yellow, and orange.

Many people visit New Hampshire to see its beautiful natural wonders.

Blueberries

Purple Lilac

Lupine

Buttercup

New Hampshire's forests and meadows are filled with many species of shrubs and wildflowers. They include blueberry, pin cherry, hobblebush, American yew, wild aster, black-eyed Susan, purple trillium, lupine, and buttercup. The official state flower is the purple lilac.

There are more than 500 species of animals scampering through New Hampshire's forestlands and meadows. Mammals include black bears, beavers, chipmunks, bobcats, little brown bats, eastern cottontail rabbits, coyotes, fishers, foxes, raccoons, skunks, shrews, squirrels, wolves, and opossums. The white-tailed deer is the official state animal of New Hampshire. Common reptiles and amphibians include bullfrogs, milk snakes, turtles, spotted newts, salamanders, and spring peepers.

Moose are very common in northern New Hampshire. Route 3 is nicknamed "Moose Alley." The scenic road runs from the town of Pittsburg, New Hampshire, to the Canadian border. It is a popular tourist spot for taking pictures of moose. Visitors are urged to drive slowly and not approach moose too closely in order to avoid accidents.

Moose are very common in New Hampshire. Many people come to photograph them.

With its many forests and wetlands, New Hampshire is a wonderful place for bird watching. The state's many bird species include bluebirds, cardinals, gulls, black-capped chickadees, ducks, eagles, falcons, hawks, geese, herons, loons, owls, and sandpipers. The official state bird is the purple finch.

The lakes and rivers of New Hampshire are teeming with fish. Common species found swimming in the state's waters include striped bass, bullhead, carp, cod, haddock, herring, mackerel, perch, pike, salmon, brook trout, walleye, whitefish, and many others. In the Atlantic Ocean waters off the state's coast are humpback, minke, and pilot whales.

New Hampshire's Loon Preservation Committee (LPC) works to protect and maintain a healthy loon population in the state.

HISTORY

People moved into the New Hampshire area after the last of the Ice Age glaciers melted, approximately 10,000 to 12,000 years ago. These Paleo-Indians were the ancestors of today's Native Americans. In time, they formed tribes that lived in villages. They planted crops such as corn, pumpkins, beans, and squash.

By the time the first European explorers arrived in the area in the early 1600s, there were two main groups of Algonquian-speaking people. These Native Americans belonged to the Abenaki and Penacook tribes.

Native Americans stand on a hill overlooking Lake Winnipesaukee.

English and French explorers visited today's New Hampshire early in the 1600s. They included English sea captain Martin Pring and French explorer Samuel de Champlain. In 1614, English explorer John Smith mapped the coast of southeastern New Hampshire.

In 1622, Captain John Mason of England was given royal permission to develop land in the New Hampshire region. He sent colonists in 1623. They built fishing and trading villages near the mouth of the Piscataqua River. In 1629, the area was officially named the Province of New Hampshire, after John Mason's English home county of Hampshire.

During its early colonial days, New Hampshire settlers took advantage of the area's rich natural resources. Fishing, lumber, and fur trading were most important. From 1641 to 1679, nearby Massachusetts controlled the land. In 1679, England's King Charles II officially made New Hampshire a separate royal colony.

Settlers soon harnessed the power of New Hampshire's rivers and streams. They built sawmills and gristmills to make lumber and flour. Shipyards were also built along the coast. New Hampshire's sturdy white pine trees were valued for making ship masts and planking.

After the French and Indian War (1754-1763), new British taxes and other hardships angered independent-minded New Hampshire citizens. War with England seemed certain. In 1774, colonists raided guns and ammunition at Fort William and Mary, which guarded the coastal city of Portsmouth, New Hampshire.

John Sullivan of the Continental Congress captured Fort William and Mary from the English in December 1774. The raiders took 200 kegs of gunpowder for the American war effort.

During the American Revolution, John Paul Jones captained the New Hampshire-built USS *Ranger*.

On January 5, 1776, New Hampshire became the first American colony to form its own independent state government and constitution. On July 4, 1776, it joined the other 12 American colonies in formally declaring independence from England.

New Hampshire's militia fought many battles during the American Revolution (1775-1783). However, there were no battles in New Hampshire itself. Several United States Navy warships and privateer vessels were built at the shipyards of Portsmouth, including the USS *Ranger*, which was commanded by naval hero John Paul Jones.

After winning independence from England, the American colonies began work on creating a new government. On June 21, 1788, New Hampshire became the ninth state to approve the United States Constitution. New Hampshire's vote made the Constitution the official law of the United States.

New Hampshire's railroads were built to move bulky goods such as lumber.

In the 1800s, New Hampshire's industries grew quickly. Textile mills sprang up along the state's waterways, and railroads were built to move bulky goods such as lumber. Many people moved to New Hampshire to find jobs. Mill towns such as Manchester prospered.

During the Civil War (1861-1865), New Hampshire sent almost 35,000 troops to fight for the Union against the Southern Confederacy. Most people in New Hampshire hated slavery. The state's soldiers fought in many major battles, including the Battle of Gettysburg in Pennsylvania.

In the decades following the Civil War, New Hampshire's economy became even more centered on manufacturing. The forests of the north were heavily logged, and granite quarries were opened. Many farms, however, struggled because of competition from other states.

The Great Depression of the 1930s hit New Hampshire hard. Many people lost their jobs, and businesses went bankrupt. Many mills and farms shut down for good.

After World War II (1939-1945), New Hampshire's economy began to rebound. Starting in the 1960s, new businesses, including many computer and electronics companies, moved into the state. Tourism also boomed as people discovered New Hampshire's natural beauty, especially the White Mountains in the north.

New Hampshire turned to tourism to help with the state's economy. Skiing became popular in the state.

DID YOU KNOW?

• In the 1600s and 1700s, when New Hampshire was an English colony, its huge, white pine trees were the property of the king. The best and straightest trees were set aside so they could be used to make masts for Royal Navy ships. Many white pines greater than 12 inches (30 cm) in diameter had royal markings carved into them. It was illegal for ordinary New Hampshire citizens to cut these trees down. Sawmills were sometimes searched to enforce the law. It caused much anger, and was one reason New Hampshire's residents were eager to declare independence from England.

The Old Man of the Mountain before and after the rocks fell on May 3, 2003.

• The Old Man of the Mountain was a famous symbol of New Hampshire. Sadly, it no longer exists. It was once a craggy outcrop on the side of Cannon Mountain, in the White Mountains of northern New Hampshire. Viewed from the proper angle, it resembled the profile of a man's face. It was a fitting symbol of the strong independence of New Hampshire's citizens. It became the state's official emblem in 1945. It even appears on New Hampshire's state quarter. In 2003, years of erosion finally caused the beloved rock formation to collapse, much to the dismay of the state's residents. Today, several plans have been offered to construct a replica or memorial near the site of the original outcropping. Someday, it is hoped, people will be able to gaze on its steadfast face once again.

DID YOU KNOW?

PEOPLE

Alan B. Shepard Jr. (1923-1998) was a naval aviator who became the second person—and the first American—to travel into space. He piloted the NASA Mercury program's *Freedom 7* capsule on May 5, 1961. Just 10 years later, in 1971, Shepard commanded the Apollo 14 Moon mission. He was the 5th person to walk on the lunar surface, and the first person to hit a golf ball on the Moon. Back on Earth, Shepard served briefly at the United Nations and was promoted to rear admiral of the United States Navy. Shepard was born and grew up in Derry, New Hampshire.

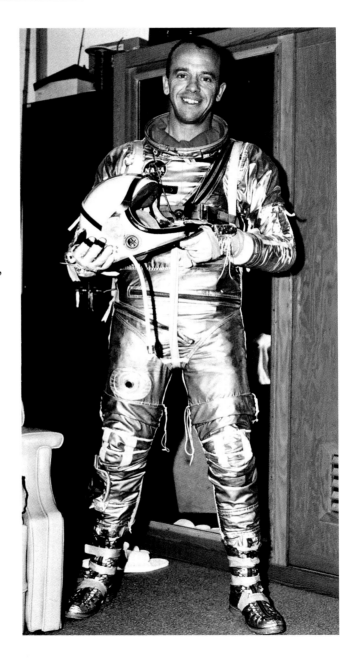

Ken Burns (1953-) is an American filmmaker best known for his documentaries about historical subjects such as the Civil War, the Lewis and Clark Expedition, jazz, and baseball. His documentary style uses historical pictures and letters narrated by actors. He has said that he tries to make people of the

past come alive through his films. His work has won many awards and honors, including two Academy Award nominations (for 1981's *Brooklyn Bridge* and 1985's *The Statue of Liberty*). Burns was born in New York, but has spent most of his adult life in New Hampshire.

Robert Frost (1874-1963) was one of America's greatest 20th century poets. His work is praised for it depiction of personal relationships, nature, and rural life, which was influenced by his many years at his farm in Derry, New Hampshire. His poems appear simple, but their meaning has great depth. Some of his most famous works include *The Road Not Taken* and *Stopping by Woods on a Snowy Evening.* Frost won four Pulitzer Prizes. The first was for his book titled *New Hampshire: A Poem with Notes and Grace Notes.* Frost was born in California, but he spent most of his life in New England, especially New Hampshire.

Daniel Webster (1782-1852) was a very influential United States politician in the mid-1800s. He represented New Hampshire in the House of Representatives. He was also a senator, and served as President Millard Fillmore's secretary of state. Webster was a skilled lawyer and a dazzling speaker who hated slavery. He believed in a strong federal government. Webster was born in Salisbury, New Hampshire.

Adam Sandler (1966-) is a popular, award-winning comedian, actor, and film producer. He worked in comedy clubs in the 1980s before earning a spot on TV's *Saturday Night Live* from 1990 to 1995. He then starred in several smash Hollywood comedies, including *Happy Gilmore*, *The Waterboy*, and *The Wedding Singer*. He has starred in dozens of films and founded his own production company. Sandler was born in New York, but grew up in Manchester, New Hampshire.

CITIES

The New Hampshire State House has been in use by the state's legislature since 1819.

Concord is the capital of New Hampshire. Its population is 42,444. Located in south-central New Hampshire, it became the capital in 1808. The city was once known for furniture making, textile mills, and granite quarries. Today, the biggest employers are state and city government, health care, and insurance. The University of New Hampshire School of Law is the only law school in the state. There are many historic buildings downtown, including the New Hampshire State House, which finished construction in 1819. The McAuliffe-Shepard Discovery Center is a space-science museum and planetarium dedicated to astronauts Christa McAuliffe and Alan Shepard, both from New Hampshire.

Manchester is the largest city in New Hampshire, and the largest city in New England north of Boston, Massachusetts. Manchester's population is 110,448. It is located in the south-central part of the state, along the banks of the Merrimack River. In the 1800s, the river provided power for the city's textile mills. Today, some of the old mill buildings are preserved. There are many finance and manufacturing businesses in Manchester. Several colleges and universities make their home in or near the city, including Southern New Hampshire University and the University of New Hampshire at Manchester. In the downtown area, there are sports stadiums, art galleries, and ethnic restaurants.

Dover is located in the southeastern corner of New Hampshire. The eastern part of the city rests along the banks of the Piscataqua River. Across the river is the state of Maine. Dover's population is 30,665. It is the 4th-largest city in the state. Settled in 1623, it is New Hampshire's oldest permanent community. Once a leading producer of textiles during the Industrial Revolution, Dover today hosts several high-technology centers, while the downtown area preserves the city's mill heritage.

Nashua is New Hampshire's second-largest city. Its population is 87,259. It is in the south-central part of the state, near the Massachusetts border. Once a fur-trading post and mill town, Nashua today has many kinds of businesses, including high-tech firms that make computers, software, and electronics. The city's historic downtown is perfect for strolling, sampling restaurants and coffee shops, window-shopping, and people watching.

Portsmouth is a historic seaport town along the Atlantic Ocean coast in southeastern New Hampshire. Its population is 21,598. Early in its history, it was a center for logging, fishing, and shipbuilding. The city was the colonial capital from 1679, but the government moved to safer locations inland during the American Revolution (1775-1783). Modern Portsmouth is home to insurance and finance companies, as well as high-technology firms and government offices. Tourists enjoy the many restaurants and shops near the historic waterfront. At Albacore Park, visitors can tour the USS *Albacore*, a research submarine used by the United States Navy to test experimental equipment.

TRANSPORTATION

There are 16,098 miles (25,907 km) of public roadways in New Hampshire. The main interstate highways are I-89, I-93, and I-95. There is also a good system of state highways that crisscross New Hampshire. They are numbered against a silhouette of the state's emblem, the Old Man of the Mountain.

The biggest airport in New Hampshire is Manchester-Boston Regional Airport. It is one of the busiest airports in New England. It handles about two million passengers each year. Other busy New Hampshire airports include Lebanon Municipal Airport and Portsmouth International Airport at Pease.

The Manchester-Boston Regional Airport is on 1,300-acres (526-ha) of land, just south of Manchester, New Hampshire.

Tugboats guide a ship into Portsmouth's Port of New Hampshire.

Nine freight railroads cross New Hampshire on 344 miles (554 km) of track. The most common bulk cargos hauled by rail include stone, cement, lumber, chemicals, food products, plus sand and gravel. Many New Hampshire citizens commute by train to the nearby Boston, Massachusetts, metropolitan area. Amtrak operates two lines that service New Hampshire, the Vermonter and the Downeaster.

The Port of New Hampshire is in Portsmouth. Located on the Piscataqua River, the busy harbor handles passenger vessels, bulk cargo, container ships, and commercial fishing boats.

TRANSPORTATION

NATURAL
RESOURCES

Early in New Hampshire's history, there were many more farms than today. However, much of the state's farmland is rocky and hilly, making it difficult to plow and harvest. In time, many farms were abandoned.

Today, there are 4,400 farms in New Hampshire. Most are small. The average farm size is just 107 acres (43 ha). Much of the land is used to grow hay, alfalfa, and corn. There is also good business in growing greenhouse and nursery plants, apples, berries, and nuts. Many farmers also harvest maple syrup. The top livestock products are poultry, eggs, and milk from dairy cows.

Hay is grown on a New Hampshire farm at the foot of the White Mountains.

The Swenson Granite Works has been in business in New Hampshire since 1883. It is one of several quarries in "The Granite State."

New Hampshire is the second-most forested state in the country, behind Maine. There is a strong demand for the state's wood products, which include kitchen cabinets, furniture, paper, flooring, and many other items. Some of the wood is used for energy production. Christmas trees are also grown in the state.

New Hampshire's nickname is "The Granite State." There are many granite quarries throughout New Hampshire, but only a few are still in operation. Sand and gravel used in construction, plus crushed stone, are more commonly mined today, especially in the Concord and Nashua areas.

NATURAL RESOURCES

INDUSTRY

In its early history, New Hampshire's economy depended greatly on textile mills and shoe manufacturing. Towns sprang up along rivers, which provided waterpower and easy transportation. In the 1920s, these industries began to decline because of competition from other states and markets overseas. Some mills were forced to shut down. Many people lost their jobs.

In the past century, New Hampshire's economy has diversified. Instead of depending on a handful of industries, there are now many kinds of companies that produce all sorts of goods. This makes it easier for the economy to remain stable, even when times are tough.

A worker loads a spool of Velcro material into a machine at the Velcro USA manufacturing facility in Somersworth, New Hampshire. Many kinds of companies produce all sorts of goods in the state.

New Hampshire's ski resorts welcome thousands of tourists to the area.

Today, New Hampshire companies manufacture machinery and electrical products. Computer-related hardware and software makers also thrive, especially in the cities of southern New Hampshire. Other manufacturing products include ball bearings, lasers, environmental pollution control systems, brushes, and pre-built homes.

Tourism is one of the biggest parts of New Hampshire's modern economy. Millions of people from all over the country have discovered the state's majestic White Mountains, national forests, pristine lakes, and ski resorts. Tourism supports approximately 62,000 jobs statewide.

SPORTS

New Hampshire has no major league sports teams. However, there are several minor league teams. The New Hampshire Fisher Cats are a Minor League Baseball team based in Manchester. They are affiliated with the Toronto Blue Jays. The Manchester Monarchs are an ice hockey team affiliated with the Los Angeles Kings. The Seacoast United Phantoms play soccer in Portsmouth.

College sports are popular in the state. Dartmouth College, in Hanover, has 33 varsity men's and women's teams that play as the Dartmouth Big Green. The New Hampshire Wildcats play for the University of New Hampshire in Durham. The Wildcats include 18 men's and women's teams.

"Gnarlz" is the mascot for the New Hampshire Wildcats.

The New Hampshire Motor Speedway has a seating capacity of 88,000 fans. The 1.058-mile (1.7-km) oval speedway is nicknamed "The Magic Mile."

The New Hampshire Motor Speedway is in the city of Loudon, near the state capital of Concord. The oval race track is nicknamed "The Magic Mile." The speedway hosts several NASCAR and motorcycle races.

Outdoor sports are big in New Hampshire, especially in the northern White Mountains region. A 161-mile (259-km) stretch of the famed Appalachian Trail winds through the state. Besides hiking and backpacking, other summer activities include camping, rock climbing, biking, canoeing, sailing, and horseback riding. There are also several popular sandy swimming beaches along the state's short Atlantic Ocean coast.

New Hampshire is famous for its winter skiing, snowboarding, and snowmobiling. Ice fishing and ice skating are also popular winter sports.

SPORTS

ENTERTAINMENT

The Mount Washington Cog Railway is a favorite tourist destination. Powered by an old steam locomotive, the train climbs to the 6,288-foot (1,917-m) summit of Mount Washington, New Hampshire's highest peak. The railway has been hauling people up the mountain for more than 150 years.

New Hampshire is famous for its many fairs and festivals. The Keene Pumpkin Festival features a tower made of hundreds of lighted jack-o'-lanterns. The New Hampshire Highland Games and Festival is held at Loon Mountain Resort in the White Mountains. It celebrates Scottish culture with bagpipes, drums, dances, heavy athletics, and sheepdog competitions.

The Mount Washington Cog Railway has been taking visitors to the summit of Mount Washington for more than 150 years.

Sailboats race on Lake Winnipesaukee, the largest lake in New Hampshire.

Lake Winnipesaukee is the largest lake in New Hampshire. Besides boating, fishing, and swimming, visitors can take lake cruises, tour historic estates and museums, and have fun at several amusement parks.

New Hampshire has many theater companies, art museums, and orchestras. Dartmouth College's Hood Museum of Art, in Hanover, features more than 65,000 works of art in its permanent collection. The University of New Hampshire's Museum of Art, in Durham, rotates its exhibitions periodically. It often includes works from New Hampshire artists.

Canobie Lake Park is an amusement park near Salem, New Hampshire. It has dozens of thrill rides, including several roller coasters and water rides.

TIMELINE

8000-10,000 BC—Paleo-Indians arrive in the New Hampshire area. They later create villages and plant crops.

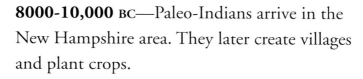

Early 1600s—Two Native American tribes dominate the New Hampshire area. They include the Abenaki and Penacook tribes.

1614—English explorer John Smith maps the coast of southeastern New Hampshire.

1622—Captain John Mason of England receives the area between the Merrimack and Piscataqua Rivers. He soon sends colonists, who build fishing and trading villages near the mouth of the Piscataqua River.

1629—New Hampshire is officially named, after John Mason's English home county of Hampshire.

1679—England's King Charles II makes New Hampshire a separate royal colony.

1741—Benning Wentworth is appointed governor of New Hampshire.

1774—American colonists successfully raid Fort William and Mary.

1776—New Hampshire becomes the first state to form its own independent state government.

1788—New Hampshire becomes the 9th state.

1808—Concord is named the New Hampshire capital.

1853—New Hampshire native Franklin Pierce becomes president of the United States.

1861-1865—The American Civil War is fought. New Hampshire stays in the Union.

1952—New Hampshire establishes the first-in-the-nation presidential primary.

2003—The Old Man of the Mountain, a granite "face" on Cannon Mountain and famous New Hampshire symbol, succumbs to years of erosion and collapses.

2015—The Dartmouth Big Green football team wins the Ivy League championship. The team finished the season with an overall record of 9-1, and an Ivy League Conference record of 6-1.

GLOSSARY

Civil War

The war fought between America's Northern and Southern states from 1861-1865. The Southern states were for slavery. They wanted to start their own country. Northern states fought against slavery and a division of the country.

Colony

A colony is the establishment of a settlement in a new location. It is often ruled by another country.

Glaciers

Huge, slow-moving sheets of ice that grow and shrink as the climate changes. During the Ice Age, some glaciers covered entire regions and measured more than one mile (1.6 km) thick.

Heavy Athletics

A series of Scottish games that require a great deal of strength. They include the caber (tree trunk) toss and hammer throw.

Industrial Revolution

A period of time starting in the late 1700s when machines began taking over many types of work that previously had been done by hand.

Lewis and Clark Expedition

Explorers Meriwether Lewis and William Clark led an expedition from 1804-1806. Called the Corps of Discovery, the expedition explored the unknown territory west of the Mississippi River.

MILITIA
Citizens who help the regular army. They are usually called for service during a military emergency.

NASA (NATIONAL AERONAUTICS AND SPACE ADMINISTRATION)
A United States government agency that started in 1958. NASA's goals include space exploration, as well as increasing people's understanding of Earth, our solar system, and the universe.

NEW ENGLAND
An area in the northeastern United States, consisting of the states of New Hampshire, Maine, Vermont, Massachusetts, Rhode Island, and Connecticut.

PRIMARY
An election of people called delegates, who choose a political candidate for office.

PRIVATEER
A privately owned and operated warship that has a government license to attack and capture enemy vessels. The government acts as a partner in the business, receiving a percentage of the profits.

WORLD WAR II
A conflict that was fought from 1939 to 1945, involving countries around the world. The United States entered the war after Japan bombed the American naval base at Pearl Harbor, in Oahu, Hawaii, on December 7, 1941.

INDEX